Original title:
Rhyme in Bloom

Copyright © 2025 Creative Arts Management OÜ
All rights reserved.

Author: Charles Whitfield
ISBN HARDBACK: 978-1-80566-634-9
ISBN PAPERBACK: 978-1-80566-919-7

Petals and Pages

In a garden where laughter grows,
Petals dance like wiggly toes.
Books stacked high, a flower bed,
Reading tales of bees who wed.

Jokes in leaves, a playful breeze,
Silly stories, if you please.
Each turn of page, a bright surprise,
Where flowers laugh and chatter rise.

Floral Expressions

Tulips wearing hats so wide,
Telling jokes with a mighty pride.
Daisies giggle at the sun,
Sharing puns, oh, what fun!

Violets sing to nearby trees,
Tickling winds and buzzing bees.
In this patch of heated laughs,
Blooms exchange their silly halfs.

The Sway of Soft Verses

Bouncing buds in cheerful rows,
Swaying gently with funny prose.
A daffodil in clownish garb,
Witty lines that charm and barb.

Lily pads with jokes to spare,
Frogs make faces, free as air.
In soft verses, laughter springs,
Nature's joy in playful flings.

Messages from the Meadow

A squirrel sends a note of cheer,
While daisies whisper, "Come, draw near!"
Every blossom, every leaf,
Teasing tales, beyond belief.

The sun winks, the shadows play,
"Look at us! We're bright and gay!"
In the meadow, giggles roam,
Nature's humor finds a home.

Syllables Among the Vines

In gardens where the grapes do swing,
A bumblebee begins to sing.
His buzzing rhymes are quite absurd,
He tells tall tales while sipping curd.

A snail with style, he takes his time,
He wears a hat, he thinks it's prime.
He dreams of speed, but just can't run,
His home is slow, but oh so fun!

A vine that thinks it's very clever,
Tripped on a leaf, oh what a endeavor!
With giggles shared among the crew,
They laugh and joke, as gardens do.

So take a seat, your drink in hand,
And laugh with us at this fine land.
For in this place where nonsense thrives,
Syllables dance and silliness dives.

Tapestry of Thorns and Thoughts

In gardens where the thorns interlace,
A hedgehog sings in a prickly place.
He pricks up ears, he knows a rhyme,
His poetry is just sublime!

A rose with sass, all dressed so bright,
Claims she's the star, the queen of night.
But with a twist, her petals twirl,
And snagged a mate, a dandelion swirl!

A witty weed joins in the play,
Composing jokes to save the day.
With laughter loud, they weave their bliss,
In tangled thoughts, they can't resist.

But watch your step as they all frolic,
For daisies are ever so symbolic!
They whisper jokes, they bloom with glee,
In thorns and laughs, they all agree.

Verses in the Meadow

In a meadow, where daisies sway,
A goat grows bored, he wants to play.
With roguish charm, he starts to rhyme,
Jumps over hills, oh what a climb!

A butterfly, with flapping grace,
Tries to dance, but loses face.
For while she twirls, she spins too fast,
And lands in mud, a funny cast!

The bunnies giggle, their tails up high,
"Come join our game!" they leap and fly.
With every hop, their laughter grows,
In grassy fields, where mischief flows.

So let's embrace this joyful cheer,
In the meadow, we have no fear!
With verses sung beneath the sun,
Together we all celebrate fun!

Symphony of Colored Leaves

A symphony of leaves in cheer,
Turns autumn wind, squawks from a deer.
With swirling reds and golds that sway,
They spin around, the leaves at play.

A squirrel dashes, claims the floor,
With acorn hats, he wants to score.
He sharpens jokes, he cracks a grin,
And all the woodland joins in the spin!

The owls go hoot, they join the tune,
As dancing foxes start to croon.
With laughter shared among the trees,
The air is filled with joyful breeze.

So let us frolic, let us cheer,
For nature's fun is always near.
In rustling leaves, we find delight,
A symphony that's out of sight!

Sonets Beneath the Canopy

Under leaf and sky so bright,
A squirrel sings with all its might.
It twirls and spins, a lively sight,
While birds all join in pure delight.

A ladybug, with polka dots,
Sips nectar from the nearest pots.
And while it hops, it chats a lot,
Oh, what a scene is this, it's hot!

The breeze winks at the trees in lace,
Each branch a dancer, full of grace.
But hold on tight, what a wild race!
This forest party, quite the place!

So if you seek a laugh or cheer,
Join nature's dance, there's nothing drear.
Beneath the greens, there's always beer,
The fun is here; let's draw it near!

The Sweetness of Stanza

In fields where candy flowers grow,
A bee with gumdrops puts on a show.
It fumbles, trips, and starts to glow,
While munching sweets, oh, what a pro!

Chocolates rain from skies above,
The worms wear hats, it's quite the love.
While butterflies like pastries shove,
And dance on cupcakes, oh so rough.

Roses tease with frosting bright,
And daisies glow with pure delight.
Each sip of soda feels just right,
As laughter echoes, taking flight.

So come along, let's celebrate,
In verse and treat, it's never late.
With sugar highs and silly fate,
We'll find our joy and animate!

Blossoms and Ballads

Down by the creek, a frog will croak,
It rhymes a tune, a funny joke.
With water lilies as its cloak,
In ripples, laughter stirs the smoke.

A rabbit hops, with style so keen,
Wears a top hat, the funniest scene.
He juggles carrots, sprightly and lean,
With every bounce, he reigns supreme.

The daisies whisper tales so bold,
Of gnomes who trade in tales told.
A friendship formed, a bond of gold,
In giggles shared, the joys unfold.

So sway beneath the boughs so wide,
With blossoms bright and joys worldwide.
Let music fill your heart inside,
For every laugh, is a joyful ride!

Where Wildflowers Sing

In meadows where the wild ones play,
The tulips tiptoe, come what may.
They giggle softly, sway and sway,
As daisies dance, inviting a stray.

A bumblebee, with glasses on,
Creates a song from dusk till dawn.
It buzzes loudly, perfect con,
While petals sway, the mood's not gone.

Hare and hedgehog share a pie,
With whipped cream clouds that seem to fly.
A fork in paw, they munch and sigh,
While daisies laugh as time goes by.

So venture where the colors bloom,
And gather 'round, dispel the gloom.
For every flower finds its room,
In laughter shared—there's always room!

Whispers of Petals

In the garden, flowers giggle,
They tickle bees that dance and wiggle.
A shy bud blinks, then starts to sway,
While daisies plot their silly play.

The tulips wear the strangest hats,
Debating if they're dogs or cats.
A rose rolled by, all out of breath,
Claiming it escaped a dance of death!

Verses in the Garden

The sunbeams joke and play hide-and-seek,
Petals laugh in colors, loud and sleek.
A daffodil sings a comic tune,
While violets gossip beneath the moon.

The bumblebees wear striped pajamas,
As butterflies pull off floral dramas.
A sunflower spins in dizzy delight,
Chasing shadows that dart out of sight.

Stanzas Under the Sun

Buttercups cheer with a giggling sound,
While lilies dance in circles, round and round.
The grass whispers secrets in a breeze,
Tickling toes and bringing sweets to tease.

The daisies clap as the wind takes flight,
Spreading jokes as the day turns bright.
A chive pretends to be a tall tree,
While pansies chuckle in harmony.

Chants of the Blossoms

Petals prance on the flower beds,
Wearing crowns made from leafy threads.
A tulip told a corny pun,
As butterflies joined in the fun.

The snapdragons snap with a laugh,
Creating mischief on the path.
In this bright patch, the blooms all play,
Making sure that dullness stays away.

Breathing in the Blooms

A flower sneezed, a petal flew,
It landed softly, right on my shoe.
I laughed aloud, what a funny sight,
Nature's humor, pure delight.

The bees wear ties, they buzz and dance,
In a garden party, they take their chance.
With pollen drinks in little cups,
They toast to sunshine, and drink it up.

A sunflower winked, I gave a grin,
It swayed and swirled, let the fun begin.
Tulips giggled in hues so bright,
As daisies spun under the light.

The breeze made jokes, it tickled my nose,
As petals twirled in garden shows.
I joined the laughter, how sweet the cheer,
In this silly world, everything's clear.

Fluttering Verses

A butterfly broke its zipper, oh dear!
It fluttered about, with nothing to wear.
With every flap, it caused a scene,
In the garden, it was quite the queen.

The daisies whispered, 'Look at that flyer!'
While marigolds cheered, 'She's such a liar!'
Her wings so bright, yet all askew,
Heckling joined in, how could it be true?

A bumblebee danced, with a skip and a hop,
"Don't dance too hard, you'll get a bee stop!"
Laughing out loud, the flowers they cheered,
In this lively plot, all worries disappeared.

From rose to lilac, a comic parade,
In a world where puns and petals invade.
So giggle along, let the humor bloom,
In leafy laughter, there's always room.

Stanzas in the Shade of Trees

Under branches wide and green,
Squirrels dance, quite the scene.
They chase their tails, then take a rest,
Nature's jesters, truly the best.

The owls hoot in a playful tune,
While rabbits hop, chasing the moon.
A leaf falls down, giving a fright,
As it lands near a sleeping kite.

Bees buzz close, in search of sweet,
Each flower's nectar, quite the treat.
They bumble about with humorous grace,
In this funny little woodland space.

The shadows flicker with glee and cheer,
As critters giggle, spreading good cheer.
So come join in this leafy play,
Where laughter echoes through the day.

Allure of Floral Cadence

In a garden where daisies twirl,
Tulips chat with quite the swirl.
Petunias gossip, sharing a laugh,
While sunflowers take a joyful path.

The roses blush as bees take notes,
While nearby pansies try out coats.
Oh what a sight in colors bright,
Nature's party, pure delight.

Violets whisper secrets so sly,
As butterflies float, oh my, oh my!
They dance to tunes only they hear,
In this garden, joy is near.

Each petal's twist is full of fun,
Under the warm and shining sun.
So come and play in this floral spree,
Where silly blooms dance wild and free.

Ballad of the Blooming Dawn

At dawn, the blooms stretch out their arms,
Yawning softly, sharing charms.
The daisies giggle, the roses blush,
In morning's warmth, there's no need to rush.

A little bud peeks out with glee,
Singing tunes to the buzzing bee.
With glances shy, they wave hello,
As morning's light begins to glow.

The lilies pirouette, full of grace,
As the morning dew drips off their face.
Caterpillars giggle, not yet a fuss,
Finding joy on a flower bus.

So let us dance as the day is drawn,
In the joyful sway of the blooming dawn.
Through laughter and blooms, we find our way,
In this silly garden, come what may.

The Aroma of Lyrical Brews

In the kitchen, pots start to sing,
Herbs dance freely, what joy they bring!
Basil declares it's the star of the stew,
While garlic grins, smelling so true.

Chives are whispering jokes quite spry,
As onions giggle, they start to cry.
Tomatoes blush, feeling quite bold,
In this aromatic tale, stories unfold.

Nutmeg spins yarns, cinnamon laughs,
While pepper sneezes, showing its gaffes.
The pot bubbles over, a hilarious brew,
As flavors mingle, creating a crew.

So come and taste, don't miss the fun,
In a kitchen where laughter has just begun.
Each aroma lifts spirits, brings cheer anew,
In this hearty kitchen, with flavors that woo.

Couplets in Color

In a garden full of cheer,
Pink polka dots appear.
Bumblebees in vibrant suits,
Dancing round in flowered boots.

Butterflies wear capes so bright,
Turning daydreams into flight.
Silly frogs croak silly songs,
While the cheeky parrot prongs.

Tulips giggle as they sway,
Tickled by a breezy play.
Dandelions puff and grin,
Making wishes from their din.

Poems from the Pollen

Bees have jokes, they buzz and hum,
Telling tales of where they're from.
With sticky hands and golden glee,
They claim they're busy, can't you see?

The daisies wiggle, wanting fun,
Debating who can run the sun.
Each petal sets a wacky tone,
As they hold court upon a throne.

Sunflowers twist, trying to pout,
If they were taller, they'd shout out.
But giggles rise like morning mist,
As blooms join in — they can't resist.

Sweet Serenades of Nature

A ladybug sings lullabies,
Underneath the painted skies.
Crickets join with tiny drums,
As nature's music softly hums.

Fragrant roses boast their flair,
Tickling noses everywhere.
They share a wink, a little tease,
With leafy pals that dance in breeze.

With every note, the flowers sway,
Exchanging puns throughout the day.
Nature's ballad, filled with cheer,
Makes the world feel warm and queer.

Ballads Beneath the Blossoms

Underneath the cherry tree,
Squirrels plot their next spree.
With acorns piled in a heap,
They giggle loud, not making sleep.

Each blossom has a silly face,
Holding secrets of the place.
The breeze whispers all around,
As petals laugh, escape the ground.

With honey drips and morning dew,
A bubbly tune flows fresh and new.
So here beneath the leafy room,
We celebrate in nature's bloom.

Melodies Under the Moonlight

In the night, the frogs do sing,
Jumping high with joy, oh what a fling!
Twirling ants on a picnic spread,
Dancing snacks to a happy thread.

The moon laughs bright, it shines so clear,
While squirrels plot their next big cheer.
A fruit pie rolls, it does a flip,
And all the critters join for a trip.

A silly cat chases its tail,
While a dog just sniffs the marvelous trail.
With wind and giggles, laughter blooms,
As stars peek in through playful flumes.

Here we sway with glee, delight,
In the glow of twinkling, silly light.
Sing creepy songs, oh what a fest,
Under the moon is where we're best.

Flourish of Ink and Daisies

A pen that spills with colors bright,
Turns simple thoughts into wondrous flight.
Daisy chains for my head, a crown,
The ink flows freely, never a frown.

On paper clouds, my dreams are drawn,
With doodles that dance from dusk till dawn.
A rabbit plays on my notebook's side,
While shooing away a tickled ride.

Pudding cups stacked in lofty towers,
Graze on words like blooming flowers.
Scribbled notes under fluffy skies,
Whispers and snickers, a sweet surprise.

The ink makes mischief, what a tease!
Each line a joke, a breeze in the trees.
With daisies twirling, laughter includes,
The fun of writing, oh how it woos!

Dances in the Glen

In the glen where critters prance,
A clumsy raccoon leads the dance.
Bunnies hop in a zigzag line,
With squirrels throwing nuts just to dine.

The mushrooms sway in silly styles,
Beneath the sun, they tease with smiles.
A hedgehog joins, it's quite a sprawl,
With giggles echoing in the call.

A flower pot spins in wild glee,
With dancing bees buzzing 'round free.
They mistake a bloom for their sweet treat,
As petals flutter near their feet.

As shadows stretch across the land,
The ground tickles, it's oh so grand.
In the glen, with each step taken,
A fun-filled dance, never shaken!

Chronicles of Petal Paths

On paths adorned with petals bright,
A squirrel tells tales of delight.
He sneaks some snacks from a picnic fair,
Inviting all to join and share.

The daisies gossip, with heads so tall,
As butterflies flutter, giving their all.
A ladybug hums an ancient tune,
While a grasshopper leaps like a cartoon.

Beneath the trees, a treasure's found,
A rubber duck spins round and round.
It quacks a story of summer days,
With hidden giggles in silly ways.

Chronicles weave through dappled light,
With every step, joy takes flight.
In a world where giggles blend,
The path of laughter shall never end.

Flora's Chorus

The daisies giggle in the breeze,
Tulips dance with utmost ease.
Sunflowers wink in golden light,
While roses blush, oh what a sight!

With every bloom, a joke they share,
Petals swipe through the fragrant air.
A bumblebee hums a silly tune,
As violets sway beneath the moon.

Each herb and stem joins in the fun,
Even weeds play hide-and-seek, just run!
Laughter sprouts from every patch,
Nature's stage, a glowing match.

So come and join this floral play,
In the garden, we'll dance all day.
With laughter sweet, we'll surely zoom,
In the joyful, jolly floral room.

Whimsy of the Wildflowers

Tiny petals with wild designs,
Chasing butterflies across the pines.
Fragrant humor fills the air,
Each wildflower seems to dare!

Dandelions blow their hints so sly,
As ladybugs buzz on by.
A daffodil tells a joke to a bee,
And they both laugh as if carefree.

Golden rods wear their goofy hats,
While critters play at hide and chats.
A clover taps its leafy toes,
Swaying to music only it knows.

In this patch of laughter bright,
Wildflowers spread pure delight.
Join the fun, don't let it slide,
Where humor blooms and good times abide!

Petals of Verse

In a garden where giggles spread,
A lilac whispers, 'Let's be wed!'
With a poppy's crown and gladdy's cheer,
They mix their tales, oh dear, my dear!

Petals of verse flutter and play,
Spilling secrets throughout the day.
The buttercups snicker, the cosmos tease,
While pansies smile in sundrenched ease.

A cactus jokes, "I've got the point!"
As zinnias wiggle, oh what a joint!
The honeysuckle hums a silly groove,
With every bloom, the laughter moves.

So gather 'round this floral spree,
Where petals flutter so playfully.
With every moment, a jest in the air,
In this joyous space, let's all share!

Whispers in the Garden

The garden chatters with tales of cheer,
From marigolds bright to violets dear.
Each whisper holds a punchline tight,
As green beans giggle with all their might.

Lettuce lolls while herbs sneak a peek,
At the wild ideas, such fun and freak!
Tomatoes chuckle in shades of red,
While zesty basil paints jokes in their head.

Cabbages roll in a leafy swirl,
As frogs leap in with a dizzy twirl.
The laughter sprouts, as ivy snickers,
In this plot, we're quite the tricksters!

So come unwind where whispers bloom,
In a garden full of giggle and gloom.
With every leaf that rustles and beams,
Listen close, for it's laughter that seems!

Cadence of the Canopy

Under the trees, the squirrels play,
Chasing their shadows, they dance away.
Leaves wear hats that flutter around,
While giggling breezes spin round and round.

A chipmunk's laugh, a parrot's quip,
Frogs leap high, but dogs just trip.
Branches wave like they're in a race,
Oh what a silly, leafy place!

A wise old owl, perched on his spot,
Tells tales of acorns that just forgot.
While mushrooms sit with cheeky grins,
Claiming they're winning at hide-and-seek spins.

The sun sneaks in with a cheeky beam,
Waking up daisies who start to beam.
A sunflower winks, a daffodil bows,
In this quirky garden, the laughter plows.

So come and join this leafy jest,
Where fun and laughter are at their best.
In the canopy's chatter, playfully loom,
Life is a giggle, all in full bloom!

Flowing Lines of Life

With each twist of the vine, a giggle unfolds,
A parrot screeches, its secrets told.
The river chuckles as it loops and bends,
Painting the banks where the garden trends.

Turtles play cards, slow and grand,
While frogs croak bets on the river's sand.
A snail throws dice with a flick of its shell,
Guessing who'll win? Oh, who can tell!

The daisies gossip, they've much to share,
About who pranced and who did dare.
Each petal whispers, a secretive bloom,
Swaying in rhythm with nature's tune.

As sunflowers sway to the farmer's song,
They dance in circles, oh so strong.
The breeze snickers, making everyone spin,
Life's a party where we all win!

So, gather around for the chuckles and glee,
Nature's the stage for you and for me.
In flowing lines, let our hearts be light,
Join the laughter from morning till night!

The Language of Leaves

Whispers and rustles, the leaves converse,
In a dialect funny, with giggles immersed.
'What's the joke?' asks a breeze on a dare,
The trees start chuckling, with rustling flair.

Their branches wave, like hands in the air,
A leaf throws shade with a spin of its hair.
'Hey, did you hear? The bark is a riot!'
Woodpeckers giggle, "Oh, we can't deny it!"

A squirrel laughs at a toppled nut,
As beetles waltz, saying "What a strut!"
Nature's own humor blooms all around,
In every nook, it joyfully's found.

Flowers join in with their colorful jest,
Creating bouquets, in style they're dressed.
The garden explodes in cheerful delight,
Where laughter and blossoms dance in the light.

So listen closely to what they say,
In the rustling leaves, find magic at play.
For humor is found in the simplest of things,
In the language of leaves, joy sweetly springs!

Symphony of the Season

The springtime chirps with a jazzy beat,
As bunnies bounce on their fluffy feet.
A caterpillar joins with its wiggle and squirm,
In this orchestra, there's no need to confirm.

The flowers chime in, a colorful tune,
With daisies bright as a sunny afternoon.
While bees play drums with their buzzing sound,
Creating a concert that's joyful and round.

Summer's arrival brings laughter galore,
As children splash and their happy hearts soar.
A picnic's unfolding, sandwiches fly,
As ants march proudly, "Just give it a try!"

Autumn brings trumpets of orange and gold,
As leaves shake loose, their stories unfold.
A joking wind twirls, a playful prank,
Sending bouquets of leaves down the plank.

In winter, the snowflakes giggle and glide,
With snowmen sporting a dapper divide.
In this symphony of seasons, so grand,
Life's a funny concert, led by nature's hand!

Rhythms of the Wild

In the jungle, monkeys swing,
They chatter loud, and loudly sing.
A parrot struts with flair and pride,
While sneaky snakes try to hide.

The elephants dance upon their feet,
With trumpets sounding, quite a treat.
A crocodile takes a silly dive,
In a splashy scene, who's still alive?

The cheetah's fast, but trips on grass,
While zebras munch, then let it pass.
A lion yawns, what a great snooze,
In the wild, you can't lose!

So join the fun, take a quick peek,
In nature's show, there's no critique.
With laughter loud, the wild remains,
In the rhythms of joy, nothing wanes.

Sonnet to the Soil

Oh, soil rich with secrets so sublime,
You cradle plants and bugs in joyful grime.
A worm wriggles, what a silly sight,
And bumbles buzz with endless delight.

With shovels, we dig, oh what a chore,
But the flowers laugh as they start to soar.
The daisies dance in the gentle breeze,
While daisies giggle behind the trees.

In muddy boots, our feet do squelch,
And every step brings forth a belch.
Oh, soil dear, your gifts we adore,
In laughter's arms, we plant and more!

As seasons change, the garden thrives,
In happy chaos, our joy derives.
From dirt, we rise with roots so deep,
In every bloom, our laughter keeps.

Lines of Lavender

Lavender sways in the softest breeze,
With bees in a frenzy, aiming to tease.
The aroma tickles, laughter it stirs,
As butterflies flutter in whimsical whirs.

A hare hops by with a curious glance,
While daisies sway, they join in the dance.
The sun peeks through, a spotlight divine,
As all the flowers wish to shine.

In pots, they chat with a cheerful hum,
Sharing secrets when they hear one come.
Petals shake hands, an odd little crew,
In lavender lines, they bring laughter too.

So stroll with glee through the garden air,
With silly blooms, we've not a care.
In every sprout and bright little hue,
There's joy waiting, just for you!

Harmonies of the Harvest

In fields of corn, the cobs all giggle,
As scarecrows dance, and roots all wiggle.
Pumpkins grin with their great big smiles,
While sunflowers sway in whimsical styles.

The apples whisper sweet, juicy tales,
While overripe pears start to sail.
Chickens cluck with a sense of flair,
In the symphony of farmyard air.

The carrots play their underground role,
As turnips shake and try to console.
With mice doing jigs on the greenest grass,
In harvest time, there's joy to amass.

So let's raise a toast to the merry ground,
Where laughter brings us all around.
In every seed, a chuckle's sown,
In harvest's embrace, we find our home.

Chronicles of Blossoming Dreams

In a garden where whispers dance,
Petals giggle at a chance.
Bumblebees buzz a silly tune,
While daisies chuckle 'neath the moon.

Gnomes are plotting pranks of cheer,
Hiding sweets and lemonade near.
Tulips wiggle with delight,
As butterflies join the flight.

Each bloom tells tales of sunshine bright,
While vines twist in pure delight.
The sun peeks in, and here we are,
Creating chaos, a floral bazaar.

With laughter sprouting all around,
Nature's jokes are quite profound.
In this patch of silly schemes,
We cultivate our laughing dreams.

The Lure of Lush Lines

Petunias pose with flair and grace,
While tulips make a pouty face.
Lilies whisper secrets low,
As violets pluck each row.

The sun paints silly shadows cast,
And daisies join in, holding fast.
While marigolds, in golden hue,
Share puns that make the garden woo.

In every corner, mischief brews,
As daffodils don wacky shoes.
They dance and twirl in vibrant hues,
While butterflies share playful views.

With every twist, the petals laugh,
Creating joy, a leafy craft.
In this plot of giggles bright,
We bloom in fun, pure and light.

A Garden's Silent Song

In the stillness, laughter quakes,
As lilacs tease with playful shakes.
Cacti smirk, all prickly smiles,
While ferns perform their leafy wiles.

In the hush, a gentle breeze,
Tickles petals, makes them sneeze.
The sunflowers wink and twirl around,
Trading whispers, giggles abound.

An oak tree drops a silly hat,
The squirrels ponder over that.
Blossoms giddy in the shade,
Release a symphony well-played.

With every rustle, secrets shared,
In this garden, laughter's declared.
Nature's joy is soft yet strong,
As blooms unite in a silent song.

The Story in Every Stem

Every stem holds tales galore,
Of raindrops, sun rays, and folklore.
A dandelion, puffed and proud,
Dreams of flying, shouting loud.

While roses poke their nose in seeds,
Planting pranks, mischievous deeds.
Marigolds trade jests with flair,
Tickling bees that buzz in air.

Each leaf holds a chuckle sweet,
As roots tap dance beneath our feet.
And every thorn, with cheeky jest,
Proclaims it's all a daring quest.

In this patch of whimsy bright,
We gather tales, both day and night.
A garden rich with joy and scheme,
That whispers softly—'Chase your dream!'

In the Garden of Stanzas

In a garden of words, we find a delight,
Where the puns grow tall, and the jokes take flight.
The daisies chuckle, as they wave from the sun,
While the snapdragons tease—always ready for fun.

Insects with jokes fly around with a grin,
A caterpillar's punchline? 'Where have you been?'
The tulips are giggling at bees in a race,
While the sunflowers cheer from their lofty high place.

When rain brings a sprinkle, they jump and they play,
Dancing in puddles like a bright cabaret.
With every new blossom, new laughter is sown,
In this whimsical place, humor's always grown.

Whispering Petals

Petals sing softly in breezy delight,
Their whispers and giggles escape into night.
A rose with a pun says, 'I'm feeling so thorny,'
While violets just laugh at their own little story.

The daisies make jokes that bring sunshine to gloom,
With each tiny bloom, watch the laughter resume.
They tease a shy bud as it opens with glee,
Saying, 'Come on now, join the fun, just be free!'

A lily tells tales of a frog in a bow,
Who danced at the pond and forgot not to crow.
In this garden of humor, where petals unite,
The joy of the flowers shines brightly at night.

The Rhapsody of Nature's Palette

Take a brush of bright colors, and splash them around,
Nature paints laughter, a symphony sound.
The daisies waltz under a rainbow so wide,
While daisies and sunflowers all dance side by side.

Crickets add beats with their chirps and their hums,
While bees do the cha-cha, how silly they come!
Their polka dots buzzing, they whirl like a dream,
In a carnival chorus, it's all quite a scene!

Petals bow low for a bow to the sun,
In the rhapsody of bloom, they're all in for fun.
With laughter and color, they grow hand in hand,
Painting joy on the canvas that's this lovely land.

Verses in Blooming Color

In a meadow of mischief, all colors collide,
Where each verse is lively, and giggles abide.
The poppies are prancing with skirts of bright red,
While the tulips tell jokes that are way out of thread.

As the wind starts to whistle a tune oh-so-fine,
The petals join in, creating a line.
Each line holds a chuckle, a twist, and a grin,
While daisies provide the occasional spin.

So let's sip sweet nectar and dance in the sun,
With verses so clever, together we'll run.
In this garden of laughter, where humor takes flight,
We bloom in bright colors from morning till night.

Lyrical Flora

In the garden where daisies dance,
A bee made a joke about his pants.
With stripes so bright, he took a stance,
Said, 'I wore them to impress, not by chance!'

Tulips giggled in hats made of cheese,
While sunflowers hummed in the teasing breeze.
'We're not just pretty, we aim to please,
Join our game, it's sure to seize!'

Petunias winked with their petals aglow,
'Let's throw a party, come on, let's go!'
But marigolds muttered, 'We're just too slow,
Can't we all just take it nice and low?'

Then violets twirled in a jolly parade,
With ferns acting coy, their plans delayed.
'Do the flirt, do the twist,' a lilac exclaimed,
In this crazy garden, we all get well played!

Echoes in the Meadow

In a meadow where giggles sprout,
A rabbit sang not knowing the route.
He tripped on a flower, spun about,
'Oops! Not my fault, I'm just full of clout!'

Butterflies blushed as they fluttered near,
'Did you hear that quack? It's bringing me cheer!
The frog thinks he's cool, but I'll make it clear,
He croaks out of tune, let's give him a sneer!'

Crickets laughed with their legs akimbo,
'We can't all be stars,' chimed the old limbo.
'But we shine in the night, if you really know,
Finding the joys in the daytime's window!'

So the flowers all joined in the festive fun,
Counting the clouds while they danced in the sun.
'Join us today, leave your troubles be done,
In this meadow, dear friends, we're never out-run!'

Melodies of Springtime

In springtime's hair of wild green curls,
A squirrel shared tales with background swirls.
He claimed his nuts could perform neat twirls,
As acorns laughed, rolling over like pearls.

Narcissus joked, flipping petals alight,
'Every flower here is quite a delight!
Do I look fabulous or slightly uptight?
I thrive on compliments, day and night!'

Daffodils danced, practicing their kicks,
'We should launch a band; we'll play some tricks.'
But daisies declined, 'We prefer real picks,
Let's savor this sunshine, nothing contradicts!'

Chirpy tunes from birds soaring high,
Joined laughter from blooms beneath the blue sky.
And all of the colors started to vie,
For fun in the springtime just surely won't die!

Bards Among the Flowers

In a circle where lilies begin to sway,
A bard told stories in a whimsical way.
With jokes made of pollen and petals on display,
Roses applauded, 'Oh, do go and play!'

Pansies chimed in with a giggly tune,
As violets rolled under the mighty moon.
'We'll burst into laughter and float like a balloon,
Chasing the stars, let's leave our cocoon!'

Daisies whispered, 'What should we wear?'
As marigolds argued from over there,
'A gown made of sunshine? Or feathers to share?'
'We need to stun! Fashion's quite rare!'

With all shades involved, they made quite the scene,
Creating a laughter like none had ever seen.
In the garden of joy, where all was serene,
Bards mingled with flowers, quite the amusing routine!

Footprints in the Floral Path

In the garden where daisies play,
I stepped on a tulip, oh what a day!
The flowers giggled, petals took flight,
As I danced in circles, what a silly sight.

Bees buzzing loudly, wearing their hats,
As I stepped on a rose, oh where are my mats?
With every misstep, the blossoms just grin,
In this floral ballet, I spin and I spin.

Frogs in the pond join in the fun,
Croaking their laughter as I start to run.
Chasing the butterflies, slipping on dew,
In this wild floral field, I've lost my shoe!

So here's to the blooms that never take blame,
For my foolish adventures, they just play the game.
With petals and laughter, I'll dance all day,
In this whimsical garden, I'll forever stay.

Garden of Stanzas

In the garden of verses, words sprout with glee,
A sunflower whispers, 'Come garden with me!'
The daisies all giggle, the roses turn red,
As I trip on a line, and fall on my head.

Worms wear their glasses, reading my prose,
While butterflies giggle at my garden clothes.
With each little stanza, I wiggle and twist,
Creating a rhythm that simply can't be missed.

In the shade of a willow, I've planted some puns,
Beneath the bright sun, we're all having fun.
Pansies are laughing, their petals all bright,
As I dabble in wordplay, a silly delight.

So come join this garden where laughter can grow,
In the soil of the silly, let your wit flow.
With stanzas as flowers, we'll dance in a row,
In the garden of laughter, let's reap what we sow!

The Sound of Sowing

In the sound of the sowing, the seeds start to sing,
The carrots are jiving, the onions bling bling.
With a hoe as my partner, we salsa in soil,
Each plant with a story, each plant with some toil.

Squirrels beat drums on the watering cans,
As I plant my new lettuce and do little dances.
The peas sway in rhythm, the corn gives a cheer,
While I whistle a tune, and snack on a beer.

Around me the flowers are tapping their feet,
While insects in top hats, put on quite a feat.
In this crazy garden, we're having a ball,
With laughter and music, we're never too small.

So here's to the sounds that gardening brings,
To the giggles of veggies and laughter that rings.
With pitchforks and spades, we'll laugh till it's night,
In the symphony blooming, everything feels right.

Petals and Prosody

With petals a-flutter, I dance through the scene,
The daisies are giggling, my outfit's a dream!
I stumble on tulips, their laughter a song,
In this whimsical garden, where I just belong.

The violets are chatting, a witty debate,
While the sunflowers sway, trying hard not to rate.
A bumblebee buzzes, with jokes that are sweet,
In the patch of the silly, we all share a seat.

So here's to the petals, all vibrant and bright,
They tickle my toes, bring joy to my flight.
With verses as flowers, I weave and I play,
In the garden of laughter, come join me today!

Echoing into the Wild

In a forest where squirrels play,
Their acorns dance, a wild ballet.
Birds tweet tunes, oh what a show,
While frogs croak as they steal the glow.

A raccoon jokes, with a sly little grin,
Stealing snacks from the trash bin.
The deer laugh, all in a row,
As the sun sets, casting a golden glow.

Trees sway gently, sharing a jest,
Leaves giggle softly; they know best.
Nature's laughter fills the bright sky,
While clouds drift by, with a playful sigh.

Amidst all, the wind whispers cheer,
Tickling petals, oh so near.
Echoes of joy in the wild so free,
A nature's joke, just you wait and see!

Nature's Sweet Sonnet

In the garden where daisies prance,
Bees wear tuxedos, ready to dance.
A butterfly flutters with glamour and flair,
While the ants march on, a comical pair.

The daisies chuckle with every breeze,
As a snail slips by with utmost ease.
Frogs in the pond throw a big splash,
Making the dragonflies giggle and dash.

Tulips stand tall, part of a play,
Their petals whispering jokes of the day.
Dandelions puff up their tiny seeds,
Spreading laughter wherever one leads.

In this sweet sonnet of playful delight,
Nature bursts forth, colors shining bright.
Each creature a player in this grand show,
A symphony of giggles, gentle and slow.

Poems Born from the Soil

Beneath the dirt where worms wiggle,
Lies a world that makes you giggle.
Seeds plot their paths with a wink and a nudge,
While sprouts dive in, they won't budge.

The potatoes laugh, hiding below,
Calling their friends, "Come join the show!"
Carrots play peek-a-boo with the sun,
Laughing together, oh what fun!

Tomatoes wear blushing coats of red,
Telling tales that sparkle in your head.
Radishes boast with their spicy sass,
While the peas sing sweetly as they pass.

In this soil where joy takes root,
Life bursts forth, a merry pursuit.
With each new sprout, the garden's a dream,
Nature's own poems, vibrant and gleam.

The Palette of Springtime Whispers

In the meadow where colors collide,
Laughter blooms wide, with nothing to hide.
Paintbrushes flutter, each flower a hue,
As daisies and violets play peek-a-boo.

Tulips giggle under the bright sun,
While butterflies flutter, their work's never done.
The wind tells secrets, soft and low,
As colors swirl in a merry show.

Birds chirp stories of what they've seen,
In this world painted bright and serene.
Each whisper of spring sings a funny tune,
Where nature's palette makes hearts swoon.

A canvas of laughter, a sight to behold,
As springtime's whispers, like stories unfold.
In this gallery of giggles, we all find delight,
Nature's own art, both whimsical and bright.

Petal-soft Murmurs

In a garden where giggles grow,
Flowers gossip, putting on a show.
Bees wear hats and dance with glee,
Who knew plants could be so free?

The daisies tell jokes, oh what a treat,
While tulips tap their tiny feet.
Sunflowers wink, they're in cahoots,
With the roses, wearing silly boots.

A bumblebee brings a cake of pollen,
"It's a party!" he shouts, and they come a-callin'.
With sprinkles of sunshine, laughter blooms,
In this garden full of fun and fumes.

So come, my friend, and join the spree,
Where petals whisper hilariously.
Laughter spruces the air anew,
In these soft murmurs, joy's the brew.

Songs of the Salted Sea

At the beach where crabs sing round,
The seashells giggle beneath the ground.
Waves tickle toes in a playful spree,
As fish hum tunes with such glee.

Seagulls squawk in off-key delight,
Wearing sunglasses, what a sight!
A dolphin spins and does a flip,
While starfish dance, they're fully equipped!

Mermaids laugh, they've got style,
With glittery tails that make you smile.
Sandy turtles join the parade,
In this salty sea, fun's never delayed.

Oh, the ocean's a wild, wacky place,
Where every wave has a comical face.
So listen close, let those songs play,
In the salty sea, we'll splash all day!

Verse of the Vibrant Wild

In the woods where the critters chat,
A squirrel's got a brand new hat.
With berries bright in a jolly feast,
He claims he's the king, at least!

The owls wear glasses, reading at night,
While raccoons plan a grand delight.
A fox writes poems, oh what a flair,
With words that dance through the cool air.

The flowers gossip, their colors bold,
Sharing tales of adventures untold.
A playful breeze sends leaves in a whirl,
In this wild, vibrant world, watch and twirl!

So come join the laughter, don't be shy,
In nature's theater, let fun soon fly.
With each little creature, the joy's on trial,
In the verse of this wild, we'll stomp in style!

Flourish of the Forgotten

In a clump of weeds, old tools reside,
A rusty rake with nothing to hide.
"Remember me?" it seems to say,
As it chuckles about the good ol' days.

The fence post creaks, sharing a jest,
Of days when it was at its best.
With vines that tickle the sky so blue,
It paints a picture, funny and true.

A gnome with a grin, and a hat too wide,
Stands guard on the lawn, full of pride.
He tells of the times when laughter flowed,
In this forgotten patch where fun's been sowed.

So lift your gaze, let the past adorn,
With whispers of joy, old blooms reborn.
In the flourish of memories still bright,
Let's dance with the shadows and join in the light!

Blooms of Narrative

In the garden of stories, where giggles sprout,
A sunflower sneezed, and the bees flew about.
A tale of a tree, with branches that dance,
Who'd steal all the hats when it got the chance.

Worms tell their tales in the soil below,
Of the time they got lost in a rainstorm's flow.
They wriggle and chuckle, quite full of glee,
At the squishy adventures by old Mr. Bee.

Petunias gossip about on the breeze,
While daisies plot schemes, aiming to tease.
With colors so bright, they prance and they play,
In this whimsical land where imagination stays.

So plant your own stories, let laughter unfurl,
In the garden of nonsense, let joy take a whirl.
With each silly petal, embrace the delight,
For the blooms of narrative are always in sight.

The Language of Leafy Tales

The leaves tell secrets, in whispers they hide,
Of a squirrel who slips, on a curious ride.
A nut in his paws, he trips with a cheer,
And lands in a puddle, soaked from ear to ear.

The branches all giggle, they wiggle and sway,
As the wind tells a tale of a mischievous day.
A ladybug danced, with shoes made of dew,
While the grass laughed aloud at the puddly view.

A mushroom decided to throw a grand ball,
Inviting the critters, both tiny and tall.
With fireflies shining, they twirled in great glee,
In the language of leaves, they were wild and free.

So listen intently to nature's own rhyme,
In the shade of the trees, lose yourself for some time.
Where laughter and stories entwine in a twirl,
And leafy tales flourish in a whimsical whirl.

Blossoming Cadence

A tulip once sang, with a voice so sweet,
It caught all the colors in a rhythmic beat.
With every bright petal, it swayed to the tune,
And made daisies dance under the light of the moon.

The bees joined the chorus, a buzzing delight,
As butterflies twirled in the soft morning light.
Their laughter like music, a carousel sound,
In the garden of joy, where giggles abound.

A fickle old fern, with a flair for the grand,
Wished to lead the dance, with a leaf-wave command.
But tripped on a gopher, who laughed in surprise,
As he tumbled and rolled under sunny blue skies.

So gather your blooms, let them sway and prance,
In this blossoming cadence, indulge in the dance.
For nature is funny, with humor so bright,
As we join in the revels, from morning till night.

Nature's Poetic Canvas

On nature's grand canvas, with colors so fair,
A valiant rose waved her long petal hair.
With every soft breeze, she twirled in delight,
While tulips would jest, 'She's a beauty, alright!'

A clever hedge named Larry told jokes to the sprout,
As they plotted a play that would leave folks in doubt.
When daisies took stage, they forgot all their lines,
And the audience giggled at their wiggly signs.

A painterly pond held reflections of glee,
With frogs all auditioning for roles in the spree.
Their chorus of croaks echoed over the glen,
A show of mishaps, again and again.

So grab a paintbrush, find joy in the hue,
In this nature's canvas, let laughter ensue.
For the art of the wild is a sight to behold,
Where stories and humor are lovingly told.

The Chorus of Cheery Blooms

In a garden where giggles sprout,
Flowers dance with a joyful shout,
Petals tease like playful sprites,
Waving 'hello' with each sunlight.

Bees are buzzing, they can't decide,
Which bloom to tickle, where to hide,
Daisies laugh at the pompous rose,
While sunflowers strike a silly pose.

Tulips twirl in a breezy waltz,
Pansies chuckle, as green grass halts,
A merry medley in full display,
With butterflies joining the fun ballet.

Symphony of Fading Light

As daylight fades, the crickets sing,
A twilight tune that makes hearts swing,
Fireflies flicker, like winking stars,
Chasing shadows, they'll never be far.

The breeze tells jokes as it sweeps past,
Rustling leaves in a giggle blast,
Crickets chirp with a twinkling tone,
Whispering secrets of the unknown.

Night falls softly, curtain of grey,
Yet laughter lingers, it's here to stay,
With every croak and hoot of night,
The fading sun wraps the world in light.

Echoes in the Evergreen

In the woods where the giggles bloom,
Pines are chuckling, dispelling gloom,
Squirrels chatter in a nutty spree,
While owls hoot their comical glee.

Branches sway in a playful jest,
The wind's a rascal that knows no rest,
Acorns drop in a clumsy dance,
Nature's folly, it takes a chance!

A thistle pricks, but it wears a grin,
"Don't mind my quills, come on in!"
The forest hums a quirky song,
With echoes of laughter all night long.

The Poetry of Pollination

Buzzing bees recite their plan,
Whirling 'round like a cheerful fan,
Pollen dusted on their fuzzy suits,
They write their verses on sweet fruits.

Ladybugs land with a gentle tap,
Joining in on this nature rap,
Ants march in with their tiny steps,
Delighted in the dance, no missteps.

Petals open, with a giggle and wink,
Inviting creatures to pause and think,
Nature's canvas, colorful and bright,
Each moment of joy a pure delight.

Verses of Vividness

In a world where socks dance, oh what a sight,
The cat wears a hat, under moonlight.
A bee with a tie buzzes past a shoe,
While flowers gossip about a dandelion too.

Jellybeans sprout in the garden so bold,
Confetti drops from trees as stories unfold.
The sun wears sunglasses, a quirky delight,
As clouds play hopscotch, oh what a night!

Bunnies pull pranks on the wise old owl,
While turtle DJs spin tunes with a growl.
Rain dances giggle in puddles so wide,
And the moon joins the fun with its silver tide.

So let's celebrate laughter and silly surprise,
In this vivid realm beneath the skies.
With every chuckle and whimsical dream,
We paint the world with a joyous gleam.

Nature's Narrative

The leaves tell tales with a swish and a sway,
Of squirrels who steal snacks and play all day.
While worms wear glasses and dig with flair,
The sun smiles down, it's a colorful affair.

Chirping crickets compose songs with zest,
While raccoons rock out, thinking they're the best.
A flower sneezes, sending seeds in flight,
In this bustling world, laughter takes flight.

Ants parade proudly, stacked in a line,
Who knew that the queen had a thing for wine?
As rain comes to help them take a big sip,
The puddles jump up for a froggy trip.

With each little giggle from creatures so small,
Nature tells stories that delight us all.
Under stars that twinkle with mischief and cheer,
We find joy in the quirks that nature holds dear.

Garden Serenade

In the garden where veggies wear caps with pride,
The carrots tell secrets the radishes hide.
Tomatoes are blushing from too much sun,
While cucumbers giggle; it's all in good fun.

The peas form a band, playing tunes from the vine,
With lettuce as backup, it's quite a fine line.
Onions cry laughter, releasing their tears,
As pumpkins roll over, sparking up cheers.

Bees with tiny banjos serenade the blooms,
While butterflies chuckle in swirling costumes.
A gopher shoots marbles, quite a cool trick,
And snails take a ride on a leaf like a slick.

Every petal and leaf in this silly spree,
Whispers of fun in the garden's jubilee.
Where joy grows in rows and laughter does sprout,
In this blissful place, there's no room for doubt.

The Poet's Bouquet

A poet stood blooming with words in a stew,
While daisies chimed in with a bright sunny hue.
Their petals were scribbling sweet rhymes in the air,
As the tulips pirouetted with fanciful flair.

Puns were the pollen, and laughter the bees,
Tickling the stanzas that danced with the trees.
A daffodil dressed up in glittery sheen,
Declared it a party, all twisty and keen.

Silly verses fluttered from lilac to rose,
Spreading giggles and grins, as the garden arose.
Witty lines tickled as they tangled and spun,
Creating a spectacle brighter than sun.

So gather your laughter, embrace every twirl,
In this whimsical world where joy loves to whirl.
For poetry blooms, with its vibrant bouquet,
Filling hearts with laughter that dances away.

Nature's Enchanted Lines

Bumblebees buzz with glee,
Tickled by petals, you see!
The daisies wink in the sun,
Their dance is just so much fun.

A squirrel wears a tiny hat,
Chasing shadows, imagine that!
With acorns as his grand feast,
He squeaks, "I'm the funniest beast!"

A butterfly tries on shoes,
Each step a new pair to choose.
In colors that make others sigh,
She twirls and spins, oh my, oh my!

At dusk when the crickets hum,
They laugh at the cat's funny bum.
In this garden, joy's the theme,
Where every laugh is a dream.

Verse Sprouts Beneath the Sun

A cactus in shades of wild green,
Spouts verses, if only he's seen!
He tells the sun jokes of the day,
In a prickly, humorous way.

The worms in the soil keep score,
As flowers giggle and implore.
"Why do daisies always joke?"
"Because they're rooted in happy folk!"

The vegetables join in the cheer,
Potatoes and peas crack jokes, oh dear!
Life's better with laughter in rows,
Even radishes wear funny clothes.

As shadows stretch long in the glade,
Nature's laughter will never fade.
Each blossom a giggle, ballooned,
In this garden, joy is cocooned.

The Parchment of Petal Dreams

Ticklish leaves rustle and shake,
As daisies plan a big cake.
"What flavor?" asks one in delight,
"We'll bake it with moonbeams tonight!"

The tulip paints tales of the past,
While roses juggle, oh what a blast!
In a world where puns take flight,
Even thorns sharp with delight.

A cactus joins the flow of the quest,
Sketching landscapes in jest, it's the best.
What stories the petals do share,
Spreading laughter through the air!

As petals fall softly to ground,
Around them, giggles abound.
In the parchment of dreams, we see,
Nature's fun in harmony!

Stanzas on the Breeze

The wind carries laughter, oh so sweet,
As clouds juggle in the sunny heat.
"What did the flower say to the bee?"
"Buzz off, I'm busy! Can't you see?"

The grass tickles toes with a sigh,
As butterflies pass, fluttering high.
"Is it me, or did they just wink?"
A chorus of giggles begins to sync.

The sun wears shades, a stylish flair,
While shadows play hide-and-seek with care.
In this garden where chuckles delight,
Nature giggles through day and night.

So let's dance with the blooms, full of cheer,
Each step is a rhythm, each laugh is near.
In stanzas on the breeze, we find,
Joy blossoms fully, nature's kind.

Ode to Sun-kissed Petals

In the garden where daisies dance,
Butterflies take their chance to prance.
With a wink and a flutter, they tease the air,
Sun-kissed petals giggle without a care.

Daffodils sport their silly hats,
While bees perform in their chubby spats.
Tulips blush as they play peek-a-boo,
In this floral circus, laughter ensues!

Caterpillars spin tales of delight,
In their leafy lounges, oh what a sight!
They munch and they munch, it's quite a riot,
Who knew that snacks could turn so spry it?

So let's toast to blooms that tickle the nose,
And let every laugh from the garden rose.
For in these petals, so bright and absurd,
The whimsical joys of nature are stirred.

Rhythm of the Orchard

In the orchard where apples sway,
Squirrels chatter in a comical way.
Beneath the branches, shadows play tricks,
As giggling fruits dodge fruit-picking licks.

The pears wear glasses, looking quite smart,
While cherries try being the best at dart.
Plums roll down hills with a wobbly cheer,
A fruit jamboree, loud and clear!

Crickets tap their tiny little feet,
Joining the dance in fruity retreat.
As wind chimes jingle in gusty delight,
An orchard of laughter from morning till night.

So lift your glasses of fresh-squeezed delight,
Here's to the fruits that make life feel light!
In every orchard, the humor thrives,
With the sweet rhythm that tickles our lives.

Lyrical Landscapes

In valleys where daisies are dressed in rhyme,
The clouds are all laughing, oh what a time!
Mountains wear smiles as they reach for the sky,
While rivers giggle and twirl as they fly.

The sun plays the trumpet, brightening the day,
While shadows join in, they waltz and sway.
The daisies debate on the best dance moves,
In this lyrical land, everyone grooves!

With the wind as a choir, the world sings along,
We revel in silliness, nothing feels wrong.
The trees throw a party with branches out wide,
Hosting a banquet of joy to abide.

So skip through the meadows with glee in your step,
For these landscapes of laughter, you can't help but pep.
In every petal and leaf, there's a tune to salute,
In this world of wonder, fun takes root!

The Verse of Verdant Fields

In the fields where the grass makes a nest,
Worms tell jokes, claiming they're the best.
The daisies roll over, laughing with glee,
As the sun paints the day, oh what a spree!

Flow'rs wear silly hats, what a sight to behold,
While butterflies flutter, their colors so bold.
The ants hold a meeting, discussing their plans,
In this verdant realm, hilarity spans!

With wind-blown whispers, the daisies gossip,
As dandelions giggle, never to stop.
The soil hums tunes beneath all that green,
In a comedic world, it's a joyous scene.

So let's frolic and tumble, no worries in sight,
For this verse of the fields is pure delight.
Every flower has laughter, with joy that unfolds,
In this charming expanse, let humor be told!

www.ingramcontent.com/pod-product-compliance
Lightning Source LLC
Chambersburg PA
CBHW072143200426
43209CB00051B/313